BURNS'S SCOTLAND

Andrew Fergus

Illustrated by John Mackay

WILLIAM BLACKWOOD
1978

First published in 1978 by
William Blackwood & Sons Ltd
32 Thistle Street
Edinburgh EH2 1HA
Scotland

821·6

FER

ISBN 0 85158 129 3

Printed at the Press of
the Publisher

Contents

Introduction

Many books have been written about the Burns Country—
the twin counties of Ayrshire and Dumfriesshire—in which
the poet passed so much of his life.

Burns's Scotland, however, extended far beyond those
narrow limits. Robert Burns knew the crowded closes of
Edinburgh almost as well as he knew the banks of the Doon
and the Nith. He also made a series of well-documented
tours with the express purpose of visiting as much of his
native land as possible. Three extensive tours covered the
Highlands and that area south of Aberdeen from which his
father came. Another tour took in the eastern half of the
Scottish Border country. Many trips along the Solway Firth
were occasioned by his work as an exciseman, and his knowledge of southern Scotland was made complete by a holiday
tour of the Galloway Highlands.

Burns's Scotland, therefore, stretches from Inverness
down to the Border. It is the purpose of this book to act as a
guide to that Scotland, linking Burns's story with the buildings and landmarks which are still to be seen. It is a peripa-
tetic biography, leading the reader from Burns's birthplace
to his mausoleum, pausing long enough at each stopping-
place to relate the main events of the poet's life in the context
in which they happened and linking the most famous of his
poems with the incidents which inspired them.

Ayr and Alloway

FOR the visitor in search of Burns there is no better place to start than in the town of Ayr. Being the county town all roads in the area lead to it, and in it the tourist will find all the amenities and comfort one expects from a popular seaside resort.

It was never the poet's home, but for the first thirty of his short thirty-seven years he never lived farther than twelve miles from it. For Burns, as a farmer, its market was the centre of his commercial and social world, and his affection for both the town and its inhabitants is clearly recorded in several of his poems:

'Auld Ayr, wham ne'er a town surpasses
For honest men and bonny lasses.'

One of the buildings of interest is the Auld Parish Kirk, where Burns was baptised and where he worshipped as a child with his parents. In its churchyard are buried several of the people mentioned in his verses.

From the kirk can be seen the old footbridge over the river. It is still in use and well repays the crossing. Standing on it, looking towards the new bridge near by, recalls the poem 'The Brigs of Ayr', in which Burns depicts the old and new bridges of the town holding a heated conversation, till, stung by the new bridge's insults, the Auld Brig retorts: 'I'll be a brig when ye're a shapeless cairn!'

It proved to be a remarkably accurate prophecy. The old bridge is still the old bridge of Burns's day. The new bridge, many years after his death, was washed away in a storm, and the present structure is a replacement.

Probably the most interesting building in the town is the old Tam O' Shanter Inn in the High Street. It contains many Burns relics, but its real attraction is that it was the setting for the long, humorous poem *Tam O' Shanter*, which Burns

'Auld Ayr, wham ne'er a town surpasses'

himself and many experts have considered his masterpiece.

It was from this very inn that Tam, the hero of the poem, set out one stormy night after a long market day's drinking. His destination was Alloway, and as we follow him there by the slightly different route taken by the modern road it will give us the opportunity to acquire at least the flavour of the poem.

As he set off that night on his grey mare, Tam had several worries on his mind.

There was his wife waiting for him at home:

'Gathering her brows like gathering storm,
Nursing her wrath to keep it warm.'

There was the storm itself. And there was also a certain indefinable eerie quality about the atmosphere. As the poet put it:

'That night a child might understand
The Deil had business on his hand.'

2

To make matters worse, almost every landmark he passed had some macabre association. However, Tam pressed on:

'Whiles holding fast his gude blue bonnet;
Whiles crooning o'er some auld Scots sonnet;
Whiles glow'ring round wi' prudent cares
Lest bogles catch him unawares. . . .'

The landmark he feared most still lay between him and his home—the old ruined church called Kirk-Alloway, which enjoyed a local reputation for being haunted. As it hove into view his worst fears were realised. The roofless building was ablaze with light and the noise of music echoed from its walls.

Eventually in Tam's drink-befuddled mind curiosity overcame fear, and he spurred his horse forward to investigate. Standing up in his stirrups to peer through one of the glassless windows he soon discovered the source of the light:

'Coffins stood round, like open presses,
That shaw'd the dead in their last dresses;
And, by some devilish cantraip sleight,
Each in its cauld hand held a light. . . .'

The music was being provided by no less a personage than the Devil himself, and dancing enthusiastically to its rhythm was a fearsome collection of witches and warlocks. As the pace increased the witches cast aside their clothes and danced on in their 'sarks' (shifts or slips). All were withered and old—at least, almost all:

'But Tam kend what was what fu' brawlie:
There was ae winsome wench and wawlie, . . .'

Her name was Nannie, and her sark, in the language of the countryside, was a trifle 'cutty', that is, short and revealing. The rest of the story is quickly told:

'And how Tam stood like ane bewitch'd
And thought his very een enrich'd; . . .
Till first ae caper, syne anither,

3

Tam tint his reason a' thegither
And roars out, "Weel done, Cutty-sark!"
And in an instant all was dark. . . .'

Scarcely had the fast-sobering Tam dug his spurs into his horse than the whole hellish legion was after him. He had one thought in his mind—the old country superstition that witches will never cross running water. If he could only reach the keystone of the old bridge over the River Doon he felt he would be safe.

As he urged his mare on to the bridge Tam knew it was going to be a close thing. The young witch, Nannie, was almost upon him, her outstretched hand making one last depairing clutch at the horse.

But the gallant mare was equal to the occasion:

'Ae spring brought off her master hale,
But left behind her ain grey tail. . . .'

'Ae spring brought off her master hale . . .'

4

As we drive into Alloway today, at the southern-most end of it is the selfsame Auld Brig over which Tam galloped in such a panic. It is a picturesque scene—with the high arch of the sixteenth-century structure spanning the placid Doon and well-kept gardens running right down to the waterside. It takes a real effort of the imagination to associate anything so peaceful with the wild scenes of the poem, but it is well worth taking the customary walk over its cobbled surface to stand on the fateful keystone, if only to admire the scene below.

Close by is Kirk-Alloway, still the same roofless pre-Reformation ruin it was on the night Tam approached it with such trepidation. In addition to the glamour the poem has cast over it, the place now has an added tourist attraction. In the little kirkyard in front of it is the grave of the poet's father, William Burnes—so he always spelled the name. It was Robert who dropped the 'e' and gave the name the monosyllabic pronunciation we use today.

On William Burnes's gravestone are carved the lines his famous son composed for him:

'O ye whose cheek the tear of pity stains,
Draw near with pious rev'rence, and attend!
Here lie the loving husband's dear remains,
The tender father, and the gen'rous friend. . . .'

The gravestone itself is the third one to lie here. The original and its successor were carried off piece by piece by souvenir hunters.

There is little doubt, however, which is the most important building in Alloway—the whitewashed, thatched-roof cottage farther up the road, which was built by William Burnes with his own hands, and in which his famous son was born.

William Burnes was not a native of the place. He was born and bred in north-eastern Scotland, in that windswept part of Kincardineshire which stretches inland from Stonehaven and is usually designated by the name of 'The Mearns'. If you want a taste of the area read Scots novelist Lewis Grassic

5

Gibbon's famous trilogy, 'A Scots Quair'. It is set right in that part of the county the Burnes family came from. They are even mentioned in it—in the sturdy, straight-from-the-shoulder language for which the Mearns folk are noted:

> 'His folk had the ups and downs of all flesh till the father of Robert Burns grew up, and grew sick of the place, and went off to Ayr, and there the poet Robert was born, him that lay with nearly as many women as Solomon did, though not all at one time.'

It was a calumny on not only Robert but on his father as well. William Burnes did not grow sick of the place. Many times in later life he told his children how heartbroken he felt on that day on which he looked back at his beloved Kincardineshire for the last time. He had been brought up on the little farm of Clochnahill, which his father tenanted. Even at the best of times it barely yielded a living, but a couple of bad summers and the repressions which followed the '45 uprising (when the north came out in force for Bonnie Prince Charlie) finally bankrupted them, and the family had to leave the farm.

Since there was little prospect of employment in Kincardineshire, William, then twenty-six years old, walked to Edinburgh where he found employment as a gardener laying out the area in the south of the city now known as The Meadows. Eventually he moved west and, after two years in North Ayrshire, finally settled in Alloway, working as a gardener on private estates.

To supplement his income he leased seven and a half acres of land in Alloway with the idea of turning it into a market garden. On this he began to build with his own hands a thatched cottage, spurred on by the thought of Agnes Brown, a farmer's daughter whom he had recently met at a fair in nearby Maybole.

He brought her home as his bride to the completed cottage in 1757. It was here too, on 25th January 1759, that his eldest and most famous son, Robert, was born. As the poet himself put it:

> ' 'Twas then a blast o' Janwar win'
> Blew hansel in on Robin.'

It blew something else in as well—the gable end of the cottage, landing it a few inches from the bed where mother and new-born infant were lying. Mother and child were bundled off to a neighbour, and William Burnes set to and rebuilt it. This time his workmanship was beyond reproach, for it still stands today, the most visited house in Scotland.

It is an excellent example of a rural working-class house of the period, with both the inhabitants and the animals housed under the one roof. The living-quarters are furnished in the manner of the time, including the box-bed in which the poet was born. In the grounds at the rear a museum has been built, housing a considerable collection of Burns relics. Among the more personal exhibits is the poet's family Bible, with births and deaths recorded on the flyleaf in his own handwriting. Other exhibits vary from the original manuscripts of many of his poems, right down to the pen used by the Queen to sign the visitors' book when she visited the cottage in 1956.

There is one other building in Alloway which should be seen by anyone who visits the village. This is the Burns Monument, Scotland's tribute—financed by public subscription—to her famous son. The site chosen was on the banks of the Doon, and few would quarrel with that. What some might quarrel with is the style of the building—Grecian and ornate and just a little out of place in its Lowland Scottish setting. It does, however, contain a fine collection of relics, including such personal items as his wife's wedding ring, Bibles presented by him to Mary Campbell (to whom he was also betrothed), and a pair of inscribed drinking-glasses gifted by him to Clarinda (Agnes Maclehose), the great love of his Edinburgh period.

Although Alloway is Burns's birthplace and possesses so many Burns relics, the poet's associations with the village were too early to have had any significant influence on his development. His real life was to be lived elsewhere. Before he reached the age of eight the family were already on the move. William Burnes acquired the lease of a nearby farm, Mount Oliphant, and, with money borrowed from his former employer, set up as a farmer.

As we return from the Burns Monument to the cottage, the road to the farm leads off to the right. Follow it across the main Ayr-Maybole road, then, at the next crossroads, turn right again and in a few more yards you arrive at Mount Oliphant.

Mount Oliphant and Kirkoswald

MOUNT OLIPHANT stands high, commanding fine views over the Ayrshire coast towards the islands of Arran and the Cumbraes. It is still farmed today, though now with a neighbouring farm.

Working in these fields during his most formative boyhood years, one feels that with such a view constantly before him Burns must have been deeply influenced by it. It is all the more surprising therefore to discover that references to the sea in his poems are rare indeed. His view of nature was the inland farmer's—landscapes he depicted with loving accuracy, but seascapes entered into his world not at all.

One possible reason was that lifting his head in these fields to admire the view was something of a luxury. The work was hard and unremitting. As the eldest son, although he was only seven, Burns was his father's chief helper.

His younger brother, Gilbert, described life at Mount Oliphant as follows:

'We lived very sparingly. For several years butcher's meat was a stranger in the house, while all the members of the family exerted themselves to the utmost of their strength, and rather beyond it, in the labours of the farm. I doubt not but the hard labour and sorrow of this period of his life was in great measure the cause of that depression of spirits with which Robert was so often afflicted through his whole life afterwards. At this time he was almost constantly afflicted in the evenings with a dull headache, which at a future period of his life was exchanged for a palpitation of the heart, and a threatening of fainting and suffocation in his bed in the night time.'

Nor were matters to improve. His father's kind-hearted former employer died, and the family now had to deal with a much less sympathetic landlord who conducted his affairs through an insolent factor. Years later, in his poem 'The Twa Dogs', Burns was to put into the mouth of the collie his own bitter memories of this period.

'I've notic'd, on our laird's court-day,—
An' mony a time my heart's been wae,—
Poor tenant bodies, scant o' cash,
How they maun thole a factor's snash;
He'll stamp an' threaten, curse an' swear
He'll apprehend them, poind their gear;
While they maun stan', wi' aspect humble,
An' hear it a', an' fear an' tremble!'

Hard though life was at Mount Oliphant there were occasional brighter periods. It was here for the first time that young Robert experienced two pleasures he was to know again and again in later life. As he himself put it; 'Thus with me began love and poetry.'

He was fourteen. She was one year younger—Nellie Kilpatrick, the daughter of a neighbour. Burns found himself paired with her in the labours of the harvest, and immediately fell under her spell. In the Mount Oliphant fields he could only gaze at her shyly, but in the evening, back at the farmhouse, he poured out his heart on paper:

'O once I lov'd a bonie lass,
Aye, and I love her still;
And whilst that virtue warms my breast,
I'll love my handsome Nell. . . .'

Not a masterpiece, perhaps, but it was a beginning, and there was even an occasional line in it which, to the discerning eye, gave promise of better things to come.

The one place to which better things never came was the farm. The only hope which kept them going was the knowledge that at the end of ten years there was a 'break' clause in the lease, which would allow them to be rid of their ruinous bargain.

Before that, however, William Burnes was anxious to complete his son's education. Robert was by no means the

10

unlettered ploughman of the legend that has grown up around him. Even in Alloway he had been sent to school. This had continued at Mount Oliphant till work and the twice daily journey made it impossible. He was later sent for a short while to board in Ayr to perfect his grammar and to learn French. Now it was decided that his education was to be rounded off with a course in mensuration and surveying at Kirkoswald, a village on the Maybole road, a few miles to the south of Mount Oliphant.

'A charming Fillette who lived next door to the school . . .'

Kirkoswald was chosen for two reasons. The village headmaster, Hugh Rodger, had an excellent reputation. Even more important, Kirkoswald was the village from which Robert's mother had come, and there were plenty of relatives still living in the vicinity who would house the young poet free of charge.

In the end Robert lodged with his uncle in the farmhouse

11

of Ballochniel. Rodger's schoolhouse, now a private house, is close by the churchyard and is marked by a commemorative plaque.

However keen the teenage Burns may originally have been on mensuration and surveying, he soon found another subject much more to his liking. As Burns himself recounts:

'A charming Fillette who lived next door to the school overset my Trigonometry, and set me off in a tangent from the sphere of my studies.'

The young lady's name was Peggy Thomson, and he was soon celebrating her in a love poem entitled 'Now Westlin Winds':

'Not vernal show'rs to budding flow'rs,
Not Autumn to the farmer,
So dear can be as thou to me,
My fair, my lovely charmer!'

Many years later, on another visit to his relatives in Kirkoswald, he was to meet Peggy again, now a married woman. He presented her with an edition of his poems, with the following lines written on the fly-leaf:

'Once fondly lov'd, and still remember'd dear,
Sweet early object of my youthful vows,
Accept this mark of friendship, warm, sincere,
Friendship! 'tis all cold duty now allows. . . .'

Although Burns's formal studies may have been neglected at Kirkoswald, his time there was not completely lost. The village was a new experience to him. At that time it was heavily involved in the smuggling trade. Its inhabitants were a racier crew than the couthie farming folk he had known at home, and Burns, fascinated, studied them enthusiastically, storing up the details for future use.

The poem *Tam O' Shanter* is set in the Alloway district, but all the colourful characters in it date from this Kirkoswald period. Tam O' Shanter himself was Douglas Graham of Shanter Farm. Souter Johnny, 'his ancient, trusty, drouthy (thirsty) crony', was the Kirkoswald souter (or cobbler), John Davidson. Shanter Farm has long since gone but the Souter's House is still there, open to the public and containing not only a collection of relics of interest to Burns enthusiasts but a fine collection of tools and implements of the period.

One last place should be visited before leaving Kirkoswald—the little churchyard, where all the people Burns knew, including those he put in his poems, now lie, their graves carefully marked for the convenience of the visitor.

From Kirkoswald Burns returned to Mount Oliphant, but the family's time there was fast drawing to a close. His father obtained the lease of a larger farm, Lochlea, farther inland near the village of Tarbolton, and with a sigh of relief the family moved the ten short miles to their new home.

Lochlea, Tarbolton and Irvine

LOCHLEA lies just outside the village of Tarbolton. The farmhouse in which the Burnes family lived is still standing, but is used now as an outhouse rather than a farmhouse. Around it lie the fields in which Robert worked from the age of eighteen to the age of twenty-five.

On the whole they were happy years, in particular the first four, which were described by Gilbert Burnes as the most contented the family ever spent together. The linen trade at that time was assuming great importance in Scotland. The neighbouring village of Tarbolton was itself heavily involved in the industry, containing about twenty mills, and the two eldest Burnes children were anxious to gain a foothold in the business by growing flax. They leased a field from their father to show him how successful this could be, and eventually so converted him to their own enthusiasm that he gave virtually the whole farm over to flax-growing.

At Lochlea Robert continued, in a slightly desultory fashion, to write poetry. An incident around the farm would sometimes inspire him. He was in the habit, for instance, of tethering a pet ewe in the field adjoining the farmhouse, and a passer-by came running in one day to tell him that the ewe had fallen into a ditch and strangled itself with the tether. Burns rushed to the field to discover the ewe in a ditch entangled in the rope, but still alive. He celebrated with a rollicking mock lament entitled 'Poor Mailie's Elegy':

> 'Lament in rhyme, lament in prose,
> Wi' saut tears tricklin down your nose; . . .'

An even greater influence than the farm at this time was the nearby village. After the hermit-like existence at Mount Oliphant a place the size of Tarbolton, almost on his doorstep, was a continual attraction to the young poet.

Visit the village today and one of the first buildings you

14

will see, carefully signposted, is the 'Bachelors' Club'. The club was started by Robert and Gilbert Burns with a few of the other young men of the village. It took the form of a debating society, and seemed to be part of a slightly self-conscious plan by the poet, now in his twenties, to educate himself in the social graces.

The Bachelors' Club, Tarbolton

A more important step taken by Burns round this time was to join the Freemasons. His first lodge was Lodge St David, Tarbolton. As with so many aspects of Scottish life there were splits and divisions even among freemasons. The Tarbolton masons broke into two distinct groups, and Burns was one of the group which went off to form the rival Lodge St James, a lodge in which he was to rise to the position of depute master.

Burns is generally considered as the bard of freemasonry. He always took his masonic activities seriously, and his membership brought him many advantages. Whenever he travelled away from home he would visit the local lodge, where he found a circle of ready-made friends, many of them influential. Even at the Tarbolton meetings he made several acquaintances who were to be extremely useful to him in later life.

The building in Tarbolton where Burns first became a mason can be seen today. It is situated in Burns Street. The successor to Lodge St James is also still standing, rebuilt on the original site and containing many masonic relics of the poet from the time when he was its depute master.

Another interesting building in the area is Willie's Mill. It lies just outside Tarbolton on the road to Lochlea and is clearly signposted. Its more proper title is Tarbolton Mill, but in Burns's day it was the home of his close friend, William Muir. Burns was a frequent visitor, looking in on his way to and from Tarbolton to enjoy its warm hospitality. His friendship with William Muir was to last well beyond the Tarbolton period. Much later; when Jean Armour (who was to become Burns's wife) was thrown out of her father's home in Mauchline because of her association with the poet, it was at Willie's Mill that she found shelter. Burns never forgot this kindness, and when Willie Muir died he wrote a touching epitaph for him, beginning:

'An honest man here lies at rest
As e'er God with His image blest. . . .'

Willie's Mill has another claim to fame. It was the setting for *Death and Dr Hornbook*, Burns's long satirical poem of the Tarbolton period. The poet described how, when he was 'toddlin' down on *Willie's mill*', he came across a figure sitting on a stone by the side of the road. It turned out to be Death, and he was complaining bitterly about a local doctor called Dr Hornbook. There was no work for his 'awfu' scythe' because the doctor's 'cures' were killing off so many people.

Tarbolton hugely enjoyed this hilarious poem, and there was no difficulty in discovering who Dr Hornbook was. A hornbook was what children learned their alphabet from—and the Tarbolton schoolmaster was John Wilson. To augment his meagre salary he ran a grocer's shop in the village and, as a sideline, added the sale of a few medicines to his other trade. His role as unofficial apothecary seems to have gone to his head a little, for very soon he was diagnosing and prescribing as well, even having a handbill printed informing his clients that if they bought medicines from his shop he would also give them free advice on their illnesses and disorders.

At a masonic meeting in Tarbolton, Burns heard him boasting a little too loudly of his prowess, and, passing Willie's Mill and the stone on his way home, had the idea for the poem. He wrote it at a sitting, and his brother Gilbert informs us that he recited it to him in its entirety the following afternoon while they were working in the fields at Lochlea. The unfortunate Wilson left Tarbolton shortly afterwards. The site of his house can still be seen in Cunningham Street.

But enjoyable though some of these escapades among the menfolk of Tarbolton were, there was another and even more attractive side to the social life Burns found there. He always had an eye for a shapely female figure, and after the isolation of Mount Oliphant Tarbolton offered almost an embarrassment of riches. He celebrated with one glorious hymn of praise:

'Green grow the rashes, O;
Green grow the rashes, O;
The sweetest hours that e'er I spend
Are spent among the lasses, O.

Auld Nature swears, the lovely dears
Her noblest work she classes, O;
Her prentice han' she try'd on man,
An' then she made the lasses, O.'

To extend his acquaintanceship among the fairer sex Burns joined a dancing academy in the village, much against

17

the wishes of his father. It created a coldness between them that was to last until his father's death.

There were many things about his eldest son which worried the stern old father at this period, not least of them being a concern about clothes which he considered to verge on foppishness. We have the evidence of the poet's closest friend in Tarbolton, David Sillars, a member of the Bachelors' Club and himself an aspiring poet, that Burns was considered as something of a village dandy: 'He wore the only tied hair in the parish, and in the church his plaid, which was of a particular colour, he wrapped in a peculiar manner around his shoulders.'

Burns himself, in verse, confirms this impression:

'My coat and my vest, they are Scotch o' the best,
O' pairs o' guid breeks I hae twa, man,
And stockings and pumps to put on my stumps,
And ne'er a wrang steek in them a', man.

My sarks they are few, but five o' them new,
Twal' hundred, as white as the snaw, man,
A ten shillings hat, a Holland cravat;
There are no' mony poets sae braw, man.'

With a young man who described his heart at the period as 'like tinder', the inevitable was bound to happen. He fell head over heels in love. The girl was Ellison Begbie, a farmer's daughter who was at the time acting as a serving-maid at Cessnock, near Lochlea. So infatuated did he become that he proposed to her, but she turned him down.

Since Begbie is hardly the most poetic of names, he used various cognomens for her in the poetry he wrote at this time, such as the Lass of Cessnock Banks, and Peggy Allison, and—in the best-known love song of the period—Mary Morison. In the poem he describes how he has tried unsuccessfully to forget her by throwing himself into the social whirl:

'Yestreen, when to the trembling string
The dance gaed thro' the lighted ha',

18

To thee my fancy took its wing,
I sat, but neither heard nor saw:
Tho' this was fair, and that was braw,
And yon the toast of a' the town,
I sigh'd, and said amang them a',
"Ye are na Mary Morison."'

The poem ends with the pathetic plea:

'If love for love thou wiltna gie,
At least be pity to me shown;
A thought ungentle canna be
The thought o' Mary Morison.'

But if one girl rejected him, others didn't. In the barley
fields around Lochlea he forgot Mary Morison more easily
than he had in the dance hall at Tarbolton. He had a passionate love affair with Annie Rankin, daughter of the farmer
at nearby Adamhill farm, and celebrated it with a rollicking
love song:

'The sky was blue, the wind was still,
The moon was shining clearly;
I set her down, wi' right good will,
Amang the rigs o' barley:
I ken't her heart was a' my ain;
I lov'd her most sincerely;
I kiss'd her owre and owre again,
Amang the rigs o' barley.

Corn rigs, an' barley rigs,
An' corn rigs are bonie:
I'll ne'er forget that happy night,
Amang the rigs wi' Annie.'

More mundane matters, however, were about to take up
the poet's attention. On the farm the decision had been taken
to go over to the growing of flax. To make any profit from it
the flax had to be dressed to prepare it for spinning. This
complicated process—heckling, as it was known—had to be

19

learned, and Robert, as the eldest son, was chosen to go off and master the difficult art.

He was sent to Irvine, in north Ayrshire, then a centre of the flax-dressing industry. One of his mother's many relatives, a Mr Peacock, ran a heckling shop there, and it was to his tender care that Robert was entrusted.

Burns worked hard, but he found flax-dressing little to his taste. He fell ill, and suffered from melancholy that verged on the suicidal. The whole affair, however, was to end halfway between comedy and tragedy. While Burns, and Mr and Mrs Peacock were bringing in the new year (1782) with the traditional Scottish carousal, the heckling shop caught fire and was burned to the ground, leaving Burns, as he remarked in a letter to a friend 'like a true poet, not worth a sixpence'.

Irvine today is a large industrial centre which has been given 'New Town' status, but it has also carefully preserved its past. Burns's lodgings can be seen at No. 4 Glasgow Vennel, in the middle of a conservation area. The site of the ill-fated heckling shop is close by.

Also worth a visit is the old parish church. Burns worshipped in it throughout his stay in the town, and his pew is still pointed out. Among the interesting graves in the churchyard is that of Burns's friend, David Sillars, who became a schoolmaster in Irvine. Sillars was also responsible for the founding of the Irvine Burns Club, one of the oldest and most active in the country. The club owns several important Burns manuscripts and a fine library of books.

Other influences of the Irvine period were to have a more lasting effect upon Burns than the unsuccessful heckling experiment. The most important of these was his friendship with a young sea-captain named Richard Brown. One memorable day the two young friends paid a visit to Eglinton Woods, just outside the town. By this time Burns had all but given up writing poetry. He had, in any case, always regarded it as a purely local activity—good enough for cutting the Tarbolton schoolmaster down to size or for celebrating one of his own amours. Now in Eglinton Woods he recited a few of his verses to Brown, and was amazed at the reaction of this sophisticated man of the world. So impressed was Brown, in fact, that he advised Burns to send his poetry to a magazine.

Burns stressed on several occasions in later life that it was this opinion which first turned his thoughts to becoming a poet in real earnest. His visit to Eglinton Woods is commemorated by a plaque on the steps at the very edge of the wood.

If Burns suffered from melancholy in Irvine he was destined to find very little to relieve it when he returned to Lochlea. His father's health had broken down completely. To make matters worse his father was involved in expensive litigation with his landlord. The lease of Lochlea had been sealed in the Scottish fashion by a clasp of the hand, which left several points in the contract far too vague. William Burnes went to law, challenging the landlord's interpretation of some of these points. It was a lawsuit which was to last the rest of his life and eventually to bankrupt him.

Burns himself has summarised his father's last tragic years in a letter to a friend:

> 'After three years' tossing and turning in the vortex of litigation, he was just saved from the horrors of jail by a consumption, which, after two years' promises, kindly stepped in and carried him away. . . . His all went among the hell-hounds that prowl in the kennel of justice.'

That anything at all was saved from the wreck was due to one of Burns's masonic brethren, a Mauchline lawyer named Gavin Hamilton. He advised Robert to claim, against his father's estate, back wages not only for himself but for every one of the other Burnes children who had worked on the farm. These claims were given precedence over the claims of other creditors, and with what little he had thus managed to salvage Burns now leased from the same Gavin Hamilton a farm called Mossgiel, near Mauchline, and moved into it with the rest of his family.

Mossgiel and Mauchline

THERE is a direct road from Tarbolton to Mauchline, and just as you reach the last mile of it the farm of Mossgiel comes into view on the left.

Mossgiel stands high and windswept on what the poet's brother Gilbert called 'a wet bottom'. It was not the best sort of land on which to carry out eighteenth-century farming methods, but in 1784 the brothers entered upon the contract in good heart and with a burning determination to succeed. Robert, as the eldest, was now for the first time head of the household, and known throughout the district as 'Young Mossgiel', in that Scottish way—still alive in many districts—which confers upon the farmer the name of the farm almost as a title.

The fields that you see from the road were his responsibility, and he worked from dawn to dusk in them for the pittance of £7 a year, which was all he ever paid himself in wages during the entire lease. Many of the minor events that happened there were written up later, in the loft above the stable which he occupied as a bedroom, into some of his finest poetry. It was in those fields that he trampled the mountain daisy and ploughed up the nest of the field mouse, episodes which inspired two of his most famous poems. Passing locals will point out not only the appropriate fields, but also, such is the enduring glamour of Burns, the exact spot where each incident occurred.

The encounter with the field mouse took place during the 'back-end' ploughing in November 1785, the second year of his occupancy. Most farmers, on turning up the nest of the field mouse, would have ploughed stolidly onwards. Burns was horrified. He watched the mouse scuttling away and the nest being scattered by the wind. He mused on the effort that had gone into the building of it, the hopes the mouse had had of spending the winter in comfort there, and its plight now that any foliage for rebuilding had long since withered.

Then, typically, he brings the theme round to the human situation:

'But Mousie, thou art no thy lane,
In proving foresight may be vain:
The best-laid schemes o' Mice an' Men
    Gang aft a-gley,
An' lea'e us nought but grief and pain,
    For promis'd joy.'

The mouse in fact, is more fortunate than the man who has just destroyed its home:

'Still thou art blest, compar'd wi' me!
The present only toucheth thee:
But, Och! I backward cast my e'e,
    On prospects drear!
An' forward, tho' I canna see,
    I guess an' fear!'

This black mood was to recur again and again in the poems written in the stable loft, brought on by the realisation that Mossgiel would never make money, and the fear that the only future that awaited him was a wretched and penniless death like his father's.

It was in moods like these that the road passing so close to his door proved most tempting. If we follow it the short distance into Mauchline we arrive in a village that probably holds more memories of Burns than any other spot in Ayrshire. Almost every stone in it has been chronicled by the poet.

Arrive at the centre of the village, Mauchline Cross, and you are immediately reminded of the 'Epistle to John Kennedy':

'Now Kennedy, if foot or horse
E'er bring you in by Mauchline Cross. . . .'

In the house next to the village's most noteworthy landmark, Mauchline Castle, lived Gavin Hamilton, the lawyer from whom Burns leased his farm. He was a friend as well as a landlord, and within the walls of his house the poet spent many happy hours.

The village church, largely rebuilt now, was also to play its part, though not always too happy a one. In Burns's day the Kirk was sternly Calvinistic and the ministers and elders ruled the village with a rod of iron, supervising the morals of its citizens and punishing transgressors with fines or by forcing them to stand on a stool on the Sabbath and be rebuked publicly before the entire congregation for their sins. Many teenage girls chose suicide rather than face this humiliation, and Burns himself was to suffer the indignity of it before his days in Mauchline were over.

'A fig for those by law protected! . . .'

Just outside the kirkyard walls stand three buildings which hold happier memories of the poet. They are the three inns which in his day dispensed whisky and good cheer to the

24

locals. Only one, Poosie Nansie's, still serves its original purpose and is today a busy hostelry. Burns made it the setting for his poem 'The Jolly Beggars', a description of a memorable night's carousing by itinerant beggars. Burns's sympathies were all with the beggars and into the poem he pours some of his wildest, most revolutionary verse:

'A fig for those by law protected!
Liberty's a glorious feast!
Courts for cowards were erected,
Churches built to please the priest.'

Near by, a little closer to Mauchline Cross, stands Nanse Tinnock's. In Burns's day it was a hostelry run by a woman of the same name, and the poet was a frequent visitor, immortalising it as the change-house in his poem 'The Holy Fair'.

The 'holy fairs'—mass open-air celebrations of communion—were well known in the religious life of eighteenth-century Scotland, and Burns lashes their hypocrisies and weaknesses without mercy. The poem is one of a series he was engaged on in a campaign against the religious practices of his day. A new and more moderate faction was beginning to make its presence felt in the Kirk. In Mauchline the movement was in its infancy, and the Kirk took stern measures against any who dared to join it. One of the local leaders of the moderates was Gavin Hamilton, and it took all his legal skill and an appeal to a superior tribunal to save himself from the wrath of Mauchline Kirk Session.

Burns was never a man to stand idly by and watch a friend being attacked. He entered the fray with gusto, scattering satiric verses left and right. Local dignitaries were lampooned, and the whole neighbourhood rocked with laughter. The most biting satire of all was reserved for the man he considered the most hypocritical of all, a Mauchline elder called Willie Fisher, whom he crucified in 'Holy Willie's Prayer'.

Willie makes some scandalous confessions to God about his own amorous adventures with certain village girls, but treats these transgressions as trifles. He then directs God's attention to the sins of other villagers, including Gavin Hamilton:

'L—d mind Gaun Hamilton's deserts;
He drinks, and swears, and plays at cartes,
Yet has so mony takin arts
   Wi' Great and Sma',
Frae G—d's ain Priest the people's hearts
   He steals awa.'

The whole merciless creed of the Calvinists is lampooned as even in his prayers Willie lashes himself into a frenzy of hatred:

'L—d in Thy day o' vengeance try him!
L—d visit them wha did employ him!
And pass not in Thy mercy by them,
   Nor hear their prayer,
But for Thy people's sake destroy them,
   And dinna spare!

But L—d remember me and mine
Wi' mercies temporal and divine;
That I for grace and gear may shine,
   Excell'd by nane!
And a' the glory shall be Thine,
   AMEN! AMEN!'

Holy Willie and many of the other Mauchline villagers who people the pages of Burns's poems now lie in the kirk-yard surrounding the village church.

The third of the hostelries in Burns's day, the Whitford Arms, stands a little farther along the road. Although no longer used as an inn its origins have been spelled out in paint on its gable wall by some later, unsung local poet:

'This is the hoose though built anew
Where Burns cam' weary frae the pleugh
To hae a crack wi' Johnnie Doo
On nichts at e'en
And whiles to taste his mountain dew
Wi' Bonnie Jean.'

26

'Bonnie Jean' was Jean Armour, daughter of a master-mason in the village, James Armour, whose house stood at the foot of the Cowgate at its junction with Howard Place. Within a year of Burns's arrival at Mossgiel he was already head over heels in love with her, but the course of their true love was most definitely never to run smooth.

James Armour objected to Burns on several counts. The £7 a year which Burns paid himself wasn't nearly enough to support a wife. As a strict Calvinist James Armour was also unlikely to be favourably impressed by the poet who had lampooned the Kirk. There was, worst of all, a scandal already associated with Burns's name. A farm servant at Mossgiel, Elizabeth Paton, had recently borne his child, and far from appearing contrite Burns had actually written a poem glorying in the fact:

'Tho' now they ca' me fornicator,
And tease my name in kintry clatter,
The mair they talk, I'm kent the better,
   E'en let them clash;
An auld wife's tongue's a feckless matter
   To gie ane fash.'

But though James Armour didn't think much of Burns, his daughter did. She risked her father's wrath by continuing to meet the poet. The young couple had devised a series of signals, and sitting at the Whitford Arms Burns could communicate with Jean at her bedroom window and arrange their meetings. The window has been preserved and can be seen at the National Burns Memorial on the outskirts of the village.

The inevitable happened. Jean became pregnant and was later delivered of twins. Burns furnished her with a written declaration, which in Scots law constituted a formal contract of marriage, but her father had the document mutilated and forced Jean to repudiate Burns.

It was the blackest moment in the poet's life. In the Kirk he had to stand and receive his public humiliation for the sin of fornication. At the same time James Armour was suing him for the maintenance of the twins and threatening to throw him into jail. In desperation Burns decided to emigrate to Jamaica.

It was at this point that a new love came into his life. Her name was Mary Campbell, but because she had been born in Argyll she was known throughout the district as Highland Mary. It is almost certain that he had known her before, for she had been a maid in Gavin Hamilton's house, but at that time she was employed in one of the local mansions, Coilsfield House. In a very short time he was asking her, in person and in verse, to join him in his plans to emigrate:

'Will ye go to the Indies, my Mary,
And leave auld Scotia's shore?
Will ye go to the Indies, my Mary,
Across th' Atlantic roar?'

To raise money for the passage he was also working on a scheme to publish his poetry.

At length Mary agreed to emigrate with him. She left her employment and was to return to her parents to settle her affairs. She would then travel to her brother's home in Greenock, where she would await Burns.

He walked with her part of the way, and they were betrothed, in the Scottish fashion of the time, by clasping hands over running water. You can see the spot where the betrothal took place by leaving Mauchline on the Ayr road and travelling the two miles to the hamlet of Failford. An obelisk marks the spot and records the story. The betrothal was further solemnised by the exchange of Bibles. The Bible, suitably inscribed, which Burns gave to Mary can be seen in the Burns Monument at Alloway.

It was the last time he was to see Mary, for she died in her brother's home in Greenock. It was a blow from which Burns was never fully to recover, and he later wrote for her his very moving 'To Mary in Heaven':

'O Mary! dear departed Shade!
Where is thy place of blissful rest?
See'st thou thy Lover lowly laid?
Hear'st thou the groans that rend his breast?'

In 1786, in the midst of his grief the first—or Kilmarnock—edition of his poems was published and was an instant success. Better still, a second, Edinburgh edition, was suggested, and so Burns went off to the capital to oversee its publication and to be lionised by the great of the land—a subject we shall return to.

For the next fourteen months, although Burns was based in Edinburgh—waiting at first for his book to appear, and then for a settlement from Creech, the publisher—he travelled extensively. He visited the Borders, the Highlands, and occasionally returned to Mauchline, where he took up again, in a desultory sort of way, the old relationship with Jean Armour. On one of his trips home he discovered that she was pregnant once more and expecting a second set of twins. (They were to die soon after birth.)

Her father, furious at her folly, had shown her the door. This time, however, he was dealing with a much more assured Burns—wide acclaim and financial reward had seen to that. Jean was found lodgings with a friend, the father was won round, and in 1788 the young couple finally made their peace with the Church.

The small house in Castle Street, where they set up home, can still be seen. Burns had, however, by this time taken up the lease of the farm of Ellisland, near Dumfries, and one of the conditions was that he should rebuild the farmhouse, which was in a ruinous condition. He departed alone to undertake the task, and it was while he was sitting in the half-built farmhouse one evening, looking with longing to the west towards Mauchline, that he wrote what has become his best-known tribute to his wife:

'Of a' the airts the wind can blaw,
I dearly like the west,
For there the bonie Lassie lives,
The Lassie I lo'e best. . . .'

Before the end of 1788 Jean had joined him in temporary accommodation, the door had been closed on the little house

29

in Castle Street, and the wild bachelor days in Mauchline were over for ever.

We shall take up the story of their life together, but before doing so it is necessary, in the next two chapters, to discuss Burns's Edinburgh associations and the story of his travels through Scotland.

Edinburgh

WHEN the Kilmarnock edition of Burns's poems was printed, Mr Laurie, the minister of Loudon parish and a friend of the poet, sent a copy to Dr Blacklock in Edinburgh. Dr Blacklock, who was blind, was himself a minor poet and much respected in the capital. His enthusiasm for the new poet was boundless. He replied to Laurie in the warmest terms, advising strongly that, the first edition now having been sold out, a second edition should be printed immediately, preferably in Edinburgh.

Burns's arrival in Edinburgh

When this letter was shown to Burns he decided to take the plunge. On 27th November 1786 he set out for the capital on

31

a borrowed horse. He slept the first night at the farm of Covington Mains in the village of Covington in Lanarkshire and rode into the capital on the evening of 29th November. Leaving his horse to be collected at the White Hart Inn on the north side of the Grassmarket, he set off in search of John Richmond, a friend he had known in Mauchline. Richmond rented a room in Baxter's Close (now demolished) in the Lawnmarket, and his landlady, Mrs Carfrae, allowed Burns to share it at a weekly charge of eighteen pence.

If the poet knew only one person in the capital when he first arrived he was soon to extend his acquaintanceship dramatically. He joined the Canongate Kilwinning Lodge of Freemasons and met two former masonic friends from Ayrshire—Sir John Whitefoord, who had been master of St James Lodge Tarbolton when Burns had been depute master, and James Dalrymple of Orangefield. These two in their turn were to introduce him to many of the most prominent citizens of the capital. Lodge Canongate Kilwinning can be seen today in St John Street (No. 182 Canongate).

The most important acquaintance Burns made through his masonic connections in Edinburgh was James Dalrymple's cousin, Lord Glencairn, who was to become one of his greatest friends and benefactors. It was a friendship that was to last till Glencairn's death, an event which the heart-broken Burns marked with one of his most touching epitaphs:

> ' "The bridegroom may forget the bride
> Was made his wedded wife yestreen;
> The monarch may forget the crown
> That on his head an hour has been;
> The mother may forget the child
> That smiles sae sweetly on her knee;
> But I'll remember thee, Glencairn,
> And a' that thou hast done for me!" '

All that, however, lay in the future. In those early weeks in Edinburgh Glencairn recommended his friend, bookseller and publisher William Creech, to handle the Edinburgh edition of Burns's poetry, and Creech duly became the poet's literary agent.

It was decided that the book should be printed by Creech's partner, William Smellie, whose printing office was in Anchor Close. Burns spent many hours sitting on a stool there, reading and correcting the proofs of his poems. Also in the close was another building in which Burns spent many hours. This was Dawney Douglas's Tavern, to which Smellie introduced him. It was the meeting place of the famous Crochallan Club, which took its name from the landlord's favourite song, 'Cro Chalein' (Colin's Cattle). The regulars of the tavern had formed themselves into a pseudo-military club, called the Crochallan Fencibles, in which the various members held mock ranks. Smellie was the adjutant, and William Dunbar, a lawyer, was the colonel. Since the main purpose of the club was drinking and the enjoying of bawdy songs and poems, Burns was a valuable asset to them, and much of the material which he composed for them has been collected under the title of *The Merry Muses of Caledonia*. Despite the bawdiness of the club Burns met many influential friends in it, including several law lords and Henry Mackenzie, the most respected figure in the Edinburgh literary scene.

Although the printing works and the tavern have now gone, Anchor Close can still be seen at No. 243 High Street.

Burns made many other friends that first winter in Edinburgh. The Duchess of Gordon, in particular, received him so wholeheartedly and accompanied him to so many balls that tongues wagged in far-off London. No door was closed to him. Even the young Walter Scott, at the age of sixteen, considered it a great honour when he was introduced to Burns at Sciennes Hill House (now part of a tenement at No. 7 Braid Place, off Causewayside), the home of Professor Adam Ferguson—a scene that was captured for all time by the artist Hardie, whose painting can be seen at the Chambers Institute in Peebles.

Young Scott meets Burns

All the lionising had its effect. When the Edinburgh edition appeared in the spring of 1787 it contained the highly flattering 'Address to Edinburgh':

'Edina! Scotia's darling seat!
All hail thy palaces and tow'rs. . . .'

But Burns was not completely blinded by Edinburgh society. Readers of the Edinburgh edition, still purring over the 'Address to Edinburgh', had only to turn a few pages to the 'Epistle to William Simson' to find a very different view of the gentry of the capital, who had let the poet Robert Fergusson die penniless and neglected in their midst:

'O Fergusson! thy glorious parts
Ill suited law's dry, musty arts!
My curse upon your whunstane hearts,
Ye Enbrugh gentry!
The tythe o' what ye waste at cartes
Wad stow'd his pantry!'

Fergusson was probably the poet who had inspired Burns most, and he had wasted no time when he arrived in Edinburgh in going to pay homage at his grave. Horrified to find it neglected and unmarked, he ordered at his own expense a tombstone, and had it engraved with an epitaph that he himself composed for it:

'No sculptured Marble here, nor pompous lay,
No storied urn nor animated Bust;
This simple stone directs pale Scotia's way
To pour her sorrows o'er the Poet's dust.'

The whole transaction cost him £5 10/-, a considerable sum to a poet who could afford only eighteen pence a week for his rent. The stone and the epitaph can be seen today in Canongate Churchyard.

Now that the Edinburgh edition of his poems had been published Burns's original reason for coming to the capital had been fulfilled, and time began to lie heavily on his hands. He had a brief but passionate affair with a serving-girl named Meg Cameron, but as the weather improved he became more and more restless to be out of the city and back into the country. To leave Edinburgh permanently was impossible until Creech paid the money due him from his poems, and this Creech seemed reluctant to do.

Burns spent part of the summer of 1787 travelling, visiting the Borders, Ayrshire and the West Highlands. On returning to the capital at the beginning of August, he made straight for Baxter's Close, only to find that the landlady had let out his half of John Richmond's room and that there was no accommodation to spare.

He went instead to another friend, fellow mason Willie Nicol, a classics master at the High School. Nicol lived in an attic room above the Buccleuch Pend, which gave access to St Patrick Square, and there Burns joined him. The Buccleuch Pend has been demolished, but its site can still be seen in Buccleuch Street.

But Burns was still restless. By the end of the month he and Willie Nicol had set off on an extended tour of the

Highlands by chaise. Scarcely had they returned than Burns was off again with another friend, Dr James Adair, on one more tour of the area. (All these trips are described in detail in the following chapter.)

When Burns returned to Edinburgh with Dr Adair in October 1787, he once more found himself without accommodation. Term time had started at the High School and Nicol, having been allocated some pupils as boarders, no longer had any room for him at the Buccleuch Pend.

Nicol suggested that their mutual friend, William Cruikshank, might put Burns up. He too was a teacher at the High School, but, being a married man with a family, he was not bound by his contract to take in pupils as boarders.

Burns thus found himself leaving the crowded closes of the Old Town and crossing the North Bridge to the orderly spaciousness of the New Town which had grown up behind Princes Street. The Cruikshanks welcomed him warmly, offering him the attic room in their top-floor flat, at No. 30 St James's Square, which he was to occupy for the rest of his stay in the city.

Although his accommodation difficulties had been solved, Burns still had problems enough to occupy his attention. Creech, his agent, seemed no nearer to settling his account. Meg Cameron, the Edinburgh serving-girl, was pregnant by him and was threatening legal action. (She was eventually to be delivered of triplets.)

The news from Mauchline was equally sombre. A letter from his brother Gilbert informed him that the farm was now perilously close to bankruptcy. Even more disturbing was the latest rumour about Jean Armour. Thanks to his brief resumption of the old relationship with her when he was back at Mauchline, it was believed she was pregnant once more.

Under the pressure of these worries Burns's health, always suspect, broke down. He was confined to bed with a bout of fever. The Cruikshanks were kindness itself, and as a token of his appreciation Burns wrote for their infant daughter one of his best-loved songs: 'A rose bud by my early walk. . . .'

Burns, in his first flush of being accepted by Edinburgh society, had cherished hopes that some well-paid post would be found for him by one of his newly made influential friends. Those hopes had long since dwindled, and now the only prospect he could see was that a fairly humdrum position might be found for him in the excise service. With this in mind he tended to cultivate the friendship of excisemen, and it was on a visit to the home of one of these, Supervisor William Nimmo, that probably the most momentous event of his Edinburgh period took place.

When Burns visited the house at Alison Square, which Nimmo shared with his sister, another person was present: Agnes Maclehose, a married woman living apart from her husband. She had been married in Glasgow, but after several years of mistreating her, her husband had gone off to Jamaica to seek his fortune. She was now living in Edinburgh with her children under the protection of her cousin, William Craig, whom Burns had met at the Crochallan Club.

Between Burns and Nancy Maclehose it was love at first sight, and before he left that evening he had received an invitation from her to call and take tea with her at her flat the following week. Burns waited in a frenzy of impatience, but he was not destined to keep the appointment. A couple of evenings before it, a drunken coachman overturned the coach he was travelling in, and Burns wrenched his ankle so badly that he was confined to bed.

Before he eventually visited Mrs Maclehose in her small flat in the General's Entry, off the Potterrow, Burns and she had already exchanged several letters. They were to be the first of a long correspondence, generally known as the Clarinda Letters, from Burns's habit of addressing her by that name, while she referred to him as Sylvander.

It was a strange love affair, passionate yet restrained. That improprieties took place is obvious from some of the letters, but Mrs Maclehose was a woman of strong Calvinistic beliefs, very conscious of her vulnerable position as a married woman, and she seems to have been more successful than most of his other loves in keeping Burns at arm's length.

Both seemed to be genuinely in love, but the affair was brought to a premature close. Quite unexpectedly Creech finally settled his account. Burns received over £500, much more than he had expected. He now had the money to solve all his pressing financial problems, and on 18th February 1788, still breathing undying love for Clarinda, he set off for Ayrshire to marry Jean Armour.

It was the end of the Clarinda affair. He wrote to her after his marriage, informing her that, when a toast to a married woman was called for, he always proposed a mysterious 'Mrs Mac', but it must have been little consolation to her. They were to meet only once again—in not too happy circumstances. While they were having their idyllic meetings, Burns, unknown to Clarinda, was also carrying on a much more physical affair with an Edinburgh serving-girl called Jenny Clow. She had a child by him, but when he walked out of Clarinda's life he walked out of Jenny Clow's as well. Much later, the poor woman, now destitute, had heard Mrs Maclehose spoken of as a friend of Burns, and had gone to her in her desperation to ask if she might get word to him of her plight.

Extremely hurt and disillusioned, Mrs Maclehose wrote to Burns and informed him of the situation. He replied, begging her to give the poor woman five shillings. He also intimated that he would be in Edinburgh on a short visit the following week, and that if Jenny Clow would get in touch with him then he would make a more substantial financial arrangement in her favour.

He put up at the White Hart Inn and, once he had attended to Jenny Clow, he paid a call on Clarinda, on the pretext of returning her five shillings. There was a reconciliation, and she told him of her plan of sailing the following month to join her husband in Jamaica. It was their last meeting. On 27th December 1791, just before she sailed to Jamaica, he sent her a farewell letter, enclosing three poems, including the one which is generally considered to be his finest love song—the last sad epitaph of their love affair, 'Ae Fond Kiss':

'Ae fond kiss, and then we sever;
Ae fareweel and then for ever!
Deep in heart-wrung tears I'll pledge thee,
Warring sighs and groans I'll wage thee.

Who shall say that Fortune grieves him
While the star of hope she leaves him?
Me, nae cheerful twinkle lights me:
Dark despair around benights me.

I'll ne'er blame my partial fancy,
Naething could resist my Nancy:
But to see her was to love her;
Love but her, and love for ever.

Had we never lov'd sae kindly!
Had we never lov'd sae blindly!
Never met—or never parted,
We had ne'er been broken-hearted.

Fare-thee-weel, thou first and fairest!
Fare-thee-weel, thou best and dearest!
Thine be ilka joy and treasure,
Peace, Enjoyment, Love, and Pleasure!

Ae fond kiss, and then we sever!
Ae fareweel, Alas, for ever!
Deep in heart-wrung tears I'll pledge thee,
Warring sighs and groans I'll wage thee.'

The house in the Potterrow in which Burns and Clarinda
met so often has been long since demolished, the site of the
General's Entry now being occupied by Marshall Street
School. There is another house in Edinburgh often referred
to as Clarinda's House. This is the one in which she lived for
the last twenty-five years of her life, after she returned from
her vain attempt at a reconciliation with her husband. It is
situated at 14 Calton Hill and is marked with a commemorative tablet.

Clarinda died in 1841 and is buried in the Canongate

Churchyard, not far from the poet Fergusson. Her grave is marked with a medallion memorial.

Visitors to Edinburgh who are interested in Burns should also visit Lady Stair's House, just off the Royal Mile, which has been turned into a museum dedicated to Burns, Scott and Stevenson.

Burns's Travels Through Scotland

The Border tour

While Burns was bogged down in his financial dealings with his agent Creech, he took the opportunity to go on several extended tours of Scotland.

The first of these was his Border tour of 1787. Patrick Miller, with whom he had become acquainted in Edinburgh, had just bought the estate of Dalswinton on the River Nith near Dumfries, and he offered to lease Burns one of the farms on the estate. Burns agreed to go and look at the farms, but asked his friend Robert Ainslie, a law student, to accompany him and turn the whole trip into a holiday tour.

Burns bought a horse, which he named Jenny Geddes, and the two friends set out in high spirits. They travelled through Gifford and over the Lammermuir Hills by way of Longformacus to Berrywell, Ainslie's home just outside the town of Duns. The house can be seen today, just off the main Berwick road on the side road to Sinclairshill.

The following morning being Sunday, Burns accompanied the family to church in Duns, where the minister preached a fire-and-brimstone sermon on obstinate sinners. Burns found himself greatly attracted to Ainslie's sister, Rachel, and, on seeing her hunting through her Bible for the text, he scribbled the following lines on a piece of paper and placed them in front of her:

'Fair maid, you need not take the hint,
Nor idle texts pursue:
'Twas guilty sinners that he meant
Not Angels such as you.'

The next day Ainslie and Burns set off again, crossing the Tweed at Coldstream, where Burns for the first time in his life set foot on English soil, and celebrated the occasion, according to Ainslie, by declaiming the last two verses of his poem, 'The Cotter's Saturday Night': 'O Scotia! my dear, my native soil. . . .'

They travelled the one mile to the village of Cornhill, then returned by way of Kelso. They visited Roxburgh Castle, and Burns was much taken by the fact that King James II had died there. The castle, now usually known as Floors Castle, lies on the B6397 about two miles north of Kelso, and a holly tree in the park marks the spot where James II was killed by a bursting cannon in 1460.

That evening they reached Jedburgh, where Burns, ever susceptible to a pretty face, fell under the spell of a local girl named Isabella Lindsay. He and Ainslie lodged in the Canongate, the building today being marked by a plaque.

From here Burns set out on a sentimental visit to Wauchope House, about fifteen miles from Jedburgh. It was the seat of Mrs Elizabeth Scott, an eccentric old lady who had sent him in Edinburgh a long verse poem, casting doubts on his ploughman origins and promising to send him a plaid to keep him warm:

'My canty, witty, rhyming ploughman,
I hafflins doubt it isna true, man,
That ye between the stilts was bred
Wi' ploughmen schooled, wi' ploughmen fed. . . .'

He responded with 'The Gude-Wife of Wauchope', which contains many revealing lines about his early ambitions:

'Ev'n then a wish (I mind its pow'r)—
A wish that to my latest hour
Shall strongly heave my breast:
That I for poor auld Scotland's sake
Some useful plan or book could make,
Or sing a sang at least. . . .'

The poet now had the pleasure of meeting the poetess and discussing poetry with her.

From Wauchope he returned to Jedburgh, where he received the freedom of the burgh and where he seized the opportunity to renew his acquaintanceship with Isabella Lindsay.

He and Ainslie then visited Dryburgh and Melrose, where Burns admired both ruined abbeys, although the weather by this time had become atrocious. They slept that night at Veitch's Inn in Selkirk. It has long since disappeared, but a plaque marks the site.

The following day saw them at Innerleithen, where they paid a visit to Traquair House, the gates of which were closed when Bonnie Prince Charlie passed through them in 1745 with the promise that they would never be opened again until the Stewarts had been restored to the throne. The house, the oldest continuously inhabited house in Scotland, still keeps its gates obstinately unopened. The inn in which Burns slept in Innerleithen has gone, but the site in High Street is marked by a plaque.

From here they started making their way back to Ainslie's home at Berrywell, dining *en route* in the village of Earlston. In former days it had been known as Ercildoune and was the birthplace of that famous Scottish seer, Thomas the Rhymer. Burns visited the ruins of his castle, the Rhymer's Tower, which can still be seen.

After a few days at Berrywell the two friends set out towards the coast. At Berwick, Burns was flattered to be recognised by Lord Errol. Even more flattering attention was to be paid to him at the nearby village of Eyemouth. There he was made a royal arch-mason of St Abbs Lodge, a fact which a plaque on the wall of the lodge proclaims. Ainslie was also made an arch-mason, but—unlike Burns and a little to his chagrin—he was asked to pay for the privilege.

After a short visit to Dunbar Burns returned to Berrywell. His friend Ainslie had to leave him to return to Edinburgh, but this gave the poet the opportunity to spend a few happy days in the company of Ainslie's sister Rachel.

Burns decided to make a short tour of England, and was accompanied part of the way by two new friends he had made, named Kerr and Hood. His route lay by way of Alnwick, Newcastle and Hexham to Carlisle. At Carlisle one night he returned slightly inebriated to his inn, to be told that his horse, Jenny Geddes, had been impounded by the mayor for straying on to corporation property. It is reported that the mayor, on discovering a little belatedly to whom the horse belonged, gave hurried orders for its immediate release with the words: "Let him have it, by all means, or the circumstances will be heard of for ages to come." He was, however, already too late. Burns had immediately sat down and composed the following lines:

> 'Was e'er puir poet sae befitted,
> The maister drunk—the horse committed!
> Puir harmless beast! tak' thee nae care,
> Thou'lt be a horse when he's nae mair [mayor].'

From Carlisle Burns travelled by way of Annan to Dumfries, where he put up at the King's Head Hotel. There a letter was waiting for him, informing him that Meg Cameron, the Edinburgh serving-girl, was expecting his child. He wrote off to his friend Ainslie, asking him to see that the girl had any money she required for her immediate needs. In his reply Ainslie informed him that he too had just become the father of an illegitimate child—a revealing commentary on the morals of the period.

At Dumfries Burns received a warm welcome and was given the honorary freedom of the burgh. He took the opportunity to visit Dalswinton Estate and to inspect several of the farms, then, finding himself so near home, he decided to return there rather than go back to Edinburgh. He travelled by way of Sanquhar, arriving back at Mossgiel on 9th June 1787.

West Highland tour

About a week after he arrived back at Mauchline from his Border tour Burns was off on his travels again. Since he kept no record and travelled alone the exact route he took is unknown, but as the area visited was the West Highlands, the home country of 'Highland' Mary Campbell, it could well have been a sentimental journey connected with her

44

memory. Tradition even suggests that he travelled to Greenock to pay his last respects at her graveside, but this theory is unsupported by any evidence. The first real knowledge of Burns's route comes from a letter he wrote to his Border tour friend, Robert Ainslie, from Arrochar on 25th June 1787:

'I am writing this on my tour through a country where savage streams tumble over savage mountains, thinly overspread with savage flocks, which starvingly support as savage inhabitants. My last stage was Inveraray—tomorrow night's stage, Dumbarton.'

The jaundiced tone of the letter probably owes something to his experience the previous day at Inveraray. The Duke of Argyll was holding a house party at Inveraray Castle, and the innkeeper, in his fawning eagerness to attend to some members of the party, apparently neglected Burns, who immediately penned the following lines:

'Whoe'er he be that sojourns here,
I pity much his case—
Unless he comes to wait upon
The Lord *their* God, "His Grace".

There's naething here but Highland pride,
And Highland scab and hunger;
If Providence has sent me here,
'Twas surely in an anger.'

From Arrochar Burns travelled by way of Luss and Loch Lomondside to Dumbarton. That this part of the journey was not without incident is revealed in a letter to his friend James Smith, a draper in Mauchline. On his trip down Loch Lomondside Burns was invited to dine at what he refers to as 'a Highland gentleman's hospitable mansion'. There is no firm evidence of where this was, but it is thought to be Cameron House, home of the Smolletts. After dinner the company danced till three in the morning, at which hour the ladies retired. The gentlemen continued to drink until six, taking time out only for a brief excursion to see the sun rise over Ben Lomond.

Burns then continued his journey, which is best described in his own words from his letter:

'My two friends and I rode soberly down the Loch side, till by came a Highlandman at the gallop, on a tolerably good horse, but which had never known the ornament of iron and leather. We scorned to be outgalloped by a Highlandman, so off we started, whip and spur. My companions, though seemingly gaily mounted, fell sadly astern; but my old mare, Jenny Geddes, one of the Rosinante family, strained past the Highlandman in spite of all his efforts with the hair halter; just as I was passing him Donald wheeled his horse, as if to cross before me and mar my progress, when down came his horse, and threw his rider's breekless [trouserless] a—e in a clipt hedge; and down came Jenny Geddes over all, and my Bardship between her and the Highlandman's horse. Jenny Geddes trod over me with such cautious reverence that matters were not so bad as might well have been expected; so I came off with a few cuts and bruises, and a thorough resolution to be a pattern of sobriety in future. . . .'

Burns's next stop was Dumbarton, where he was made an honorary citizen. His burgess ticket can be seen at the Municipal Buildings. That his name does not appear on the burgh roll is attributed to the fierce opposition of the then parish minister, the Revd James Oliphant, whose previous charge had been in Kilmarnock, where Burns had lampooned him mercilessly in his satirical poem, 'The Ordination'.

From Dumbarton Burns travelled home by way of Glasgow, Paisley and Kilmarnock to Mauchline.

The second Highland tour
On his return to Edinburgh in August 1787, Burns and his new friend William Nicol planned a more extensive tour, but this time by chaise rather than on horseback.

46

They set out on 25th August and travelled by way of Corstorphine, Kirkliston and Winchburgh to Linlithgow, where Burns admired the old palace and the room where 'the beautiful injured Mary, Queen of Scots, was born'. He slept that night at the Cross Keys Inn at Falkirk. The site is today occupied by a shop and a bust of the poet.

The following morning he and Nicol visited Carron, but, since it was Sunday, they were refused admission to the famous ironworks. Burns took immediate revenge with some scathing verses:

'We cam na here to view your warks,
In hopes to be mair wise,
But only, lest we gang to hell,
It may be nae surprise. . . .'

The Carron furnace manager, himself an amateur poet, took up the cudgels in defence of the company and replied in kind:

'Six days a week to you and all,
We think it very well,
The other, if you go to church,
May keep you out of Hell.'

From Falkirk Burns and Nicol travelled by way of Larbert and Dunipace to Bannockburn, the scene of the great Scottish victory over the English in 1314. There Burns admired 'the hole where glorious Bruce set his standard', the famous borestone which can still be seen today.

The two friends slept that night in Stirling in James Wingate's Inn in King Street—now named the Golden Lion Hotel. Burns went to look at the old castle and, when he saw the state of disrepair into which it had been allowed to fall, he returned to the inn and wrote the following lines with a diamond stylus on a pane of glass:

'Here Stewarts once in triumph reigned,
And laws for Scotland's weal ordained;
But now unroofed their palace stands,
Their sceptre's swayed by other hands;

47

Fallen, indeed, and to the earth
Whence grovelling reptiles take their birth,
The injur'd Stewart line is gone,
A race outlandish fill their throne;
An idiot race, to honour lost;
Who know them best despise them most.'

They were dangerous sentiments to be expressing so publicly about the reigning house of Hanover!

The following day Burns and Nicol travelled to Harvieston, near Dollar, where his hostess was the stepmother of Gavin Hamilton, Burns's Mauchline friend. They slept the night there, and next morning went with the family to visit several beauty spots in the area, including Rumbling Bridge, Caldron Linn and the Devil's Mill.

Burns and Nicol continued their tour by way of Crieff, and then by Sma' Glen to visit Ossian's grave. A large stone near the River Almond still marks the site.

A visit followed to Taymouth Castle, the home of Baron Breadalbane, who was mentioned by Burns in the preface to his poem 'Address to Beelzebub'. The castle is still standing, but is now used as a school. While in the area Burns expressed his appreciation of the scenery by writing, in pencil, a few lines over the mantelpiece of the inn at Kenmore:

'The Tay meand'ring sweet in infant pride;
The palace rising on its verdant side;
The lawns wood-fring'd in Nature's native taste;
The hillocks dropt in Nature's careless haste. . . .'

From Kenmore they followed the Tay to Dunkeld, crossing the river by General Wade's bridge at Aberfeldy, where Burns composed his well-known 'Birks of Aberfeldy':

'Let Fortune's gifts at random flee,
They ne'er shall draw a wish frae me;
Supremely blest wi' love and thee
In the Birks of Aberfeldy.

48

Bonny lassie, will ye go,
Will ye go, will ye go,
Bonny lassie, will ye go
To the Birks of Aberfeldy?'

They continued to follow the Tay to the village of Inver, where they were housed for the night by friends, Dr and Mrs Stewart. Neil Gow, the famous Scottish fiddler, was a native of Inver, and next day he met Burns and played for him. Many of the tunes to which Burns's songs are set come from Gow's music.

Meeting Neil Gow at Inver

From Inver Burns and Nicol travelled to Blair Atholl, pausing at the Pass of Killiecrankie to visit the stone which marks the spot where Viscount Dundee was killed at the moment of his great victory. Arriving at Blair Atholl they were welcomed to Blair Castle by the Duchess of Atholl. The Duke arrived later and pressed them to stay on. They stayed two days, visiting spots of interest in the neighbourhood. Burns was introduced to Robert Graham of Fintry, one of the Scottish Commissioners of the Excise, an introduction which was to prove useful to him later when he decided to enter the excise service.

The tour was now continued by way of Dalwhinnie to Aviemore, where the snow among the hills lay eighteen feet deep in patches. Shortly afterwards they arrived in Macbeth country, and on a visit to Castle Cawdor Burns was intrigued to have pointed out to him the very bed in which King Duncan was murdered by Macbeth.

When the pair arrived in Inverness that night they put up at the Ettles Hotel, but Burns was so exhausted that he had to request the Provost to postpone a meeting which he had arranged.

From Inverness Burns took the opportunity to visit some of the local beauty spots, including the Falls of Foyers, where he was inspired to write a poem beginning:

'Among the heathy hills and ragged woods
The foaming Fyers pours his mossy floods. . . .'

The falls can still be seen today, but they are a less impressive sight since part of their water power has been diverted for use at the nearby aluminium works.

The following day the pair traversed Culloden Moor. There is a tradition that Burns's grandfather was an active Jacobite, and Burns himself often expressed Jacobite sympathies. Here he was on the very spot where the Jacobites had suffered their final tragic defeat under their leader, Bonnie Prince Charlie. It should have been one of the highlights of his tour, but all Burns recorded in his journal was: 'Come over Culloden Moor—reflected on the field of battle.'

Burns and Nicol now travelled through Nairn and Forres to Elgin, where Burns admired Elgin Abbey, comparing it to Melrose Abbey, which he had seen on his Border tour. They finally arrived at Fochabers, where Burns left Nicol at the local inn and hurried to Castle Gordon, the home of the Duke and Duchess of Gordon, with whom he had become friendly in Edinburgh. He was greeted warmly and invited to stay the night. Nicol was also included in the invitation, but when Burns went to fetch him he found him in a foul temper. Nicol insisted that they should turn down the invitation, which Burns eventually did most unwillingly, softening the blow by writing for the Gordons a poem in celebration of the castle:

'Give me the stream that sweetly laves
The banks by Castle Gordon. . . .'

They now went by way of Banff, Old Deer and Peterhead to Aberdeen, where they stayed at the New Inn in Castle Street. Burns was introduced to Bishop Skinner, son of the author of 'Tullochgorum', which Burns once described as 'the best Scotch song ever Scotland saw'.

The next day they moved south to Stonehaven. This part of the tour Burns had been looking forward to with great eagerness because it took him into the district from which his father had come and in which many of his relatives still lived.

In Stonehaven he met his cousin Robert Burnes, a lawyer, whom he described in his journal as 'one of those who love fun, a gill, a punning joke, and have not a bad heart'. Robert's wife he described as 'a sweet hospitable body, without any affectation of what is called town-breeding'. In a letter home to his brother Gilbert, he gave details of some of the other relatives he met:

'I spent two days among our relations and found our aunts, Jean and Isbal [his father's sisters], still alive and hale old women. John Caird [who married the third sister, Elspeth], though born the same year with our father, walks as vigorously as I can; they have had several letters from his son in New York. William Brand [the husband of Isbal] is likewise a stout old fellow.'

After Stonehaven Burns and Nicol travelled south and slept that night in Laurencekirk. The poet's stay is commemorated by a plaque on the Gardenstone Arms Hotel.

The following day he was in Montrose where he met his cousin, James Burnes.

As a change from their usual method of travel Burns and Nicol took a fishing smack from Auchmithie, a little fishing village near Montrose, and sailed along the wild rocky coast, landing at Arbroath, where Burns much admired the stately ruins of Arbroath Abbey.

At Arbroath they picked up their chaise again, and travelled by way of Dundee and the picturesque Carse of Gowrie to Perth. From there they paid a visit to Scone Palace where Scottish Kings were traditionally crowned. Burns was particularly impressed by Queen Mary's bed, noting in his journal that the hangings were 'wrought with her own hand'.

That night Burns slept at Kinross, but not too well, for he records that he had 'a fit of the colic'. The next day was the last of the tour, and the journal ends a little baldly with the following entry: 'Come through a cold barren Country to Queensferry—dine—cross the Ferry, and come to Edinburgh.'

The two friends had spent twenty-two days on the tour and travelled some 600 miles.

The Peggy Chalmers tour

A couple of weeks after his return from his second Highland tour Burns was on his travels once more. Creech, his agent, seemed no nearer settling his account. Meg Cameron, the Edinburgh girl pregnant by him, was threatening to go to law. There was no reason why he should stay in the capital, yet, without the money from his Edinburgh edition, he could not return home to Mauchline. He therefore decided on another tour.

This tour was not motivated, as the others had been, by his desire to see his native land and kindle his muse at some of its better known beauty spots. His reason for travelling on this occasion was much more basic. Once again he was in love.

52

The object of his affections was Peggy Chalmers, a cousin of his Mauchline landlord and close friend Gavin Hamilton. It is possible that he had known her in his Mauchline days, because she had been brought up near the village. Since then, however, her father had died, and she and her mother had come to live in Edinburgh, where Burns had frequently been in her company. From time to time Peggy also went to live with her bachelor uncle, John Tait, at his country home, Harvieston, which Burns had visited on his second Highland tour, although Peggy Chalmers was not in residence on that occasion.

This time she was in residence and, taking advantage of the standing invitation he had received on his previous visit to call whenever he was in the area, Burns set out. He chose as his travelling companion another Ayrshireman, a young doctor named James Adair. Burns kept no record of the tour, but Adair fortunately wrote up an account of it in later life.

The pair set out at the beginning of October 1787, following roughly the same route that Burns had travelled with Nicol. They went by way of Linlithgow to Carron, where the poet on this occasion managed to view the great ironworks which he had been unable to see on his previous visit. They dined the first evening at Stirling, and Burns seized the opportunity to smash the inn window on which he had scratched the anti-Hanoverian lines on his previous visit. On maturer reflection he realised that the existence of these lines lampooning the reigning house could scarcely be the best recommendation for someone like himself who hoped eventually to be offered a government position.

By a strange coincidence one of the first people Burns met in Stirling was Willie Nicol, who happened to be in town on a visit. Both were overjoyed at the chance meeting, and the rest of the evening was spent in carousing and singing.

The following morning Burns and Adair travelled from Stirling through the picturesque valley of the Devon to Harvieston, where they were very warmly received. For eight ecstatic days Burns wooed Peggy Chalmers, wrote verses to her, and visited the local beauty spots in her company. Most of them he had already visited on his previous tour, but that mattered little. He had eyes only for Peggy. In the end he proposed to her, and to his chagrin she turned him down.

Writing to her later Burns summed up his feelings very clearly:

> 'When I think I have met with you, and I have lived more of real life with you in eight days than I can do with almost anybody I meet with in eight years—when I think on the improbability of meeting you in this world again—I could sit down and cry like a child.'

The poems he wrote at that time express exactly the same emotions. For example:

> 'The tyrant death with grim controul,
> May seize my fleeting breath,
> But tearing Peggy from my soul
> Must be a stronger death. . . .'

They were emotions which were to last. Years later, bowed down with illness and in the last month of his life, he sent off his last love song to his publisher. Its title, 'Fairest Maid On Devon Banks', leaves us in no doubt to whom it was written, and it harps back to the old theme:

> 'Full well thou knowest I love thee dear,
> Could thou to malice lend an ear?
> O did not Love exclaim, "Forbear,
> Nor use a faithful lover so." . . .'

To rub salt into Burns's wounds during the Harvieston visit, his companion, Dr Adair, who had arrived fancy-free, immediately fell in love with Peggy's cousin, had his love returned, and was eventually to marry her two years later.

Leaving Adair to his happiness in Harvieston Burns made two short visits on his own—to Sir John Ramsay of Ochtertyre in Kincardineshire, and to Sir William Murray of the less well-known Ochtertyre near Crieff. Burns had been introduced to Sir William Murray by the Duchess of Gordon on his visit to Blair Castle. At Ochtertyre he was introduced to Sir William's strikingly beautiful niece Euphemia, known locally as 'the Flower of Strathmore', and promptly celebrated the occasion by writing the song 'Blythe, blythe and merry was she'.

Reunited once more with Adair, Burns next paid a visit to Clackmannan Tower, the home of an elderly lady named Mrs Catherine Bruce, who claimed to be the last of the direct line descended from the great Robert the Bruce. Burns was fascinated when she produced the sword and helmet which had belonged to the hero-king. Seeing his interest, old Mrs Bruce took the sword and knighted him. She pointed out that it was only a mock ceremony, but added drily that, being as Jacobite and anti-Hanoverian as Burns himself, she had a better right to confer titles than 'some people'.

Clackmannan Tower can still be seen on a hill to the west of Clackmannan on the A907. Since Burns's day it has fallen into ruins, but is now being restored.

From Clackmannan Burns and Adair made their way homewards, stopping at Dunfermline to admire the abbey. In the abbey church Burns's eyes lit on the cutty stool (or stool of repentance), exactly like the one he himself had to stand on in the Mauchline Kirk and be lectured publicly for his sin of fornication with Jean Armour. In light-hearted mood he now made Adair mount the cutty stool while he himself, from the pulpit, delivered a parody of the lecture which the Reverend 'Daddy' Auld had delivered on that fateful morning in Mauchline.

Before leaving the abbey Burns sought out the traditional site of the grave of Bruce and bent down to kiss the flagstones. The grave, then unmarked, is now covered with a brass plaque.

From Dunfermline Burns and Adair returned to Edinburgh by way of Queensferry, arriving back in the capital on 20th October.

Ellisland, Dumfries and Brow Well

LEAVE Dumfries on the busy A76, and in six miles a well-signposted road on the right leads you to the farm of Ellisland, nestling in a delightful situation on the banks of the Nith. It is still farmed today, although the house which Burns built is no longer used as the farmhouse. It serves instead as the home of a resident custodian who is ready at all reasonable times to show the visitor round the building and its collection of Burns relics.

When Burns moved in during the summer of 1788 the farmhouse was in a ruinous condition, and one of the clauses of his lease was to make it habitable. He camped in a dilapidated hovel on the edge of the farm and happily settled down to rebuilding the house. Jean travelled from Mauchline to join him in December, but it was the following spring before the farmhouse was finally completed, and the family moved in for Burns's last attempt at farming.

Knowledgeable friends had warned him even before he signed the lease that in his selection of the picturesquely situated Ellisland he was making a poet's rather than a farmer's choice, but he set out with high hopes. He ran it as a mixed farm, he himself attending to the arable side of it, while Jean supervised the dairy. Many of the stresses that had so troubled him at Mossgiel had lifted. His obscurity, for instance, was no longer a problem. He had tasted fame in Edinburgh, and much of it still clung to him. This made him acceptable to the finest circles of society in the neighbourhood, and he made many influential friends.

Among the best were his neighbours at Ellisland, the Riddells of Friars Carse. Stand at the farmhouse at Ellisland looking north, and you can see their well-wooded estate. So friendly did Burns become that he was given his own key to allow him to enter the estate whenever he wished. It was a privilege he used to the full, spending many happy hours musing and writing in a beautiful little hermitage the Riddells had built on the estate.

Burns also made friends among the humbler families in the area, and played his full part in the community. The nearest village was Dunscore, on the other side of the Dumfries road. Burns went to church there, and he also helped to start a reading-club and lending-library in the village. Some of the books from it are still on display in the farmhouse at Ellisland.

Many of the villagers were also to find themselves—not always to their great joy—immortalised in verse. One unfortunate in Dunscore, for instance, had an ugly wife:

'She has an e'e, she has but ane,
The cat has twa the very colour;
Five rusty teeth forbye a stump,
A clapper tongue wad deave a miller;
A whiskin beard about her mou,
Her nose and chin they threaten ither:
Sic a wife as Willie had—
I wad nae gie a button for her!'

Other more important works were to follow, for despite the difficulty of farming Ellisland it was certainly to prove a rich soil for poetry. It was here, for instance, that his masterpiece, *Tam O' Shanter*, was written. Riddell, his neighbour at Friars Carse, was host to an English antiquarian called Grose, who was touring the country collecting material for a book on Scottish antiquities he hoped to publish. Burns was invited to meet him, and suggested for inclusion in his book the old ruined church at Alloway which he remembered so well from his childhood. Grose promised to include the church if Burns would supply a few verses to go with it.

Next day Burns did no work on the farm. Instead, armed only with his walking cane, he walked up and down the banks of the Nith and wrote *Tam O' Shanter* in the course of a single day. The walk, known as Shanter Walk, is still pointed out at Ellisland.

Standing on Shanter Walk you can see the field in which Burns had an encounter which inspired another poem, 'A Wounded Hare'. Burns himself explained the circumstances in a letter to a friend in Edinburgh:

'One morning lately, as I was out pretty early in the fields sowing some grass seeds, I heard the burst of a shot from a neighbouring plantation, and presently a poor little wounded hare came crippling by me. You will guess my indignation at the inhuman fellow who would shoot a hare at this season, when all of them have young ones. Indeed there is something in that business of destroying for our sport individuals in the animal creation that do not injure us materially, which I could never reconcile to my ideas of virtue.'

The person who wounded the hare, James Thompson, son of a neighbouring farmer, puts it more succinctly: 'She ran bleeding past Burns; he cursed me and ordered me out of his sight, else he would throw me into the water.'

That evening, however, Burns's indignation spilled over in a more poetic form:

'Go live, poor wanderer of the wood and field,
The bitter little that of life remains. . . .'

It was here in Ellisland too that he wrote what is probably the most sung song in the English-speaking world, 'Auld Lang Syne', a nostalgic harping back to old times and old friends:

'We twa hae paidl'd in the burn
Frae morning sun till dine:
But seas between us braid hae roar'd
Sin' auld lang syne.

For auld lang syne, my dear,
For auld lang syne,
We'll tak' a cup o' kindness yet
For auld lang syne.'

If the poetry was going well, however, the farm certainly was not. In well under two years of starting at Ellisland he was already writing to his friend, Mrs Dunlop: 'My farm is a ruinous bargain, and would ruin me to abide it.'

It might be worth pausing at this point to reflect on the genius the Burns family seemed to have for striking 'ruinous bargains'. Mount Oliphant, Lochlea, Mossgiel, Ellisland— all were to end in disaster. Reading some biographies, with their constant tales of 'ungrateful soil', the reader could be forgiven for thinking that we are talking of some bleak Highland moor or windswept Shetland isle. It is with a start that we remember we are not talking of the Highlands or the Shetlands, but of Ayrshire and Dumfriesshire, two of the richest farming areas in Britain. All of the Burns farms are still farmed to this day, apparently yielding a comfortable enough living. It is true that farming methods have changed, and that modern drainage, in particular, has helped, but one still cannot escape the conclusion that even by the standards of their own times the members of the Burns family were spectacularly and consistently unsuccessful as farmers.

However, before taking on the farm at Ellisland, Burns had added another string to his bow. He had taken a short course of instruction to make him eligible for the excise service as soon as a vacancy presented itself. Now, in his hour of need, a vacancy did arise. He cut down drastically on the arable side of the farm, gave it over almost completely to dairying, which Jean could supervise, and took up his part-time duties as exciseman at a salary of £50 a year.

The duties of an exciseman corresponded roughly with those of the Customs and Excise Department today. One of his main functions was to ensure that the proper duty was paid on any excisable goods imported from abroad. Being based at Dumfries, Burns's beat was the picturesque Solway Firth which, owing to its relative isolation and also its proximity to the Isle of Man, was a prime target for contraband of all kinds. It was Burns's task to keep a sharp lookout for such smuggling activities. Another of his responsibilities was to ensure that the proper duty on excisable liquor was not being evaded by people distilling their own whisky, and much of his time was taken up with the tracking down and destroying of illicit stills.

For a poet who had sung so enthusiastically of the joys of whisky it was a sad comedown. Burns had no illusions about the unpopularity of the job—'looking down auld wives' barrels', as he referred to it contemptuously. His precise attitude to the post he revealed when breaking the news of it in a letter to his friend Ainslie:

> 'I know not how the word exciseman . . . will sound in your ears. I, too, have seen the day when my auditory nerves would have felt very delicately on this subject; but a wife and children have a wonderful power in blunting these kind of sensations.'

Burns found his relief in poetry. One of his most rollicking songs tells of the wonderful day when the Devil came fiddling through the town, linked arms with the local exciseman, and danced off with him. The reaction of the townspeople was ecstatic:

> 'We'll mak our maut and we'll brew our drink,
> We'll laugh, sing and rejoice, man!
> And mony braw thanks to the meikle black deil
> That danc'd awa wi' th' Exciseman.
>
> The deil's awa, the deil's awa,
> The deil's awa wi' th' Exciseman,
> He's danc'd awa, he's danc'd awa,
> He's danc'd awa wi' th' Exciseman!'

Despite his misgivings Burns seems to have settled in fairly well as an exciseman, and before very long his salary was being raised to £70 a year. It was just as well. Ellisland was now proving a total disaster. The conditions of the lease specified that at the end of three years he was to begin paying an extra £20 a year in rent, thus bringing the figure up to £70—exactly what he was earning from his excise duties! Burns realised that there was no way in which he could

'The deil's awa' wi' th' Exciseman . . .'

possibly afford to pay this amount. The only solution lay in giving up the farm. He sold off his stock and his implements by auction, and in December 1791 he bade farewell to Ellisland for ever, having sunk into it almost all of the money he had managed to save from the Edinburgh edition of his poems.

Since Dumfries was the headquarters of his excise division it was to this town that he took his family, securing the let of a small house near the lower end of the Bank Vennel (now called Bank Street). The house is still standing but is in private hands. It bears a plaque which reads: 'Robert Burns, the national poet, lived in this house with his family on coming to Dumfries from Ellisland, 1791.'

For a farmer moving to the unfamiliar surroundings of a town, the Bank Vennel had many advantages. It lies just off that broad esplanade known as the Whitesands. Today it is used as a vast parking area for the buses and cars bringing visitors to the town, but in Burns's day it was the venue of the large cattle markets for which Dumfries was famous, and ensured the poet the company of farmers whenever he felt the desire for it. Another attraction was that the same River Nith which flowed past Ellisland was still only a stone's throw away. It was a little wider here, it is true, but in many ways it was just as picturesque.

Burns and Jean at Whitesands, Dumfries

Town life also brought its disadvantages. Farming, Burns was soon to discover, had had its compensations. For the first time in his married life he found himself having to pay out money for his oatmeal, milk, butter and cheese, commodities which up till then he had taken for granted.

62

Another problem was that the accommodation in the Bank Vennel soon proved too cramped for his growing family, but that difficulty at least he could solve. He moved to the house in Mill Brae, in which he was destined to spend the rest of his life. The street is now known as Burns Street, and the two-storey red sandstone house is by far the most visited building in Dumfries. It is laid out as a Burns museum, and contains many relics. Of particular interest is the room in which Burns died.

Burns worked hard at his excise duties. Even minor promotions in the service brought fairly spectacular salary increases, and he was confident that, with the influential friends he had acquired through his poetry, it was only a matter of time before he would be promoted to a position which would put him beyond financial worry for the rest of his life.

It wasn't to be. The event that was to be his undoing had already burst like a thunderbolt upon Europe. Every poetry lover remembers how Wordsworth greeted the French Revolution: 'Bliss was it in that dawn to be alive. . . .' If that kind of reaction was produced in a relatively staid poet like Wordsworth one can imagine the effect of the Revolution on a wayward, rebellious character like Burns. One of the best known poems of his Dumfries period was his great egalitarian hymn, 'A Man's a Man for A' That':

'Ye see yon birkie ca'd a lord,
Wha struts, and stares, and a' that,
Though hundreds worship at his word,
He's but a coof for a' that:
For a' that, and a' that,
His ribband, star, and a' that;
The man of independent mind
He looks and laughs at a' that. . . .'

A poet who could express dangerous sentiments like that was unlikely to be overcautious in his praise of the French Revolution, even when the beheading of the royal family turned most of his countrymen against the revolutionaries.

Even worse, he translated his words into actions. He and several of his colleagues had apprehended a smuggling brig in the Solway Firth, and its contents were to be sold by auction. Burns bought two of its cannon and sent them to France. There was an immediate inquiry into his loyalty by the excise service, which forced him in desperation to send a humiliating letter to his friend, Graham of Fintry:

'I have been surprised, confounded and distracted by Mr Mitchell, the collector, telling me that he has received an order from your Board to inquire into my political conduct, and blaming me as a person disaffected to government. Sir, you are a husband—and a father. You know what you would feel to see the much-loved wife of your bosom, and your helpless, prattling little ones, turned adrift into the world, degraded and disgraced. . . .'

He was eventually cleared, but the dreams of high promotion had vanished for ever.

If his work in the excise brought Burns little satisfaction there were other consolations to be found in Dumfries. In the hostelries of the town he rediscovered the easy good fellowship he had known in the taverns of Mauchline and Edinburgh. His favourite 'howff' (drinking place) was the Globe Inn just off the High Street. He had known it since the days he used to visit it as a farmer coming into market from Ellisland, and it did not have the happiest of associations.

In it Burns, as susceptible as ever, had grown overfriendly with one of the barmaids, Anna Park, the pretty blonde niece of the landlady. The inevitable happened, and she bore him a child. Burns accepted this fairly philosophically, taking the baby home to his wife, Jean, with the request that she bring it up as one of the family. Jean, remarkable woman that she was, seems to have accepted the request almost as philosophically, merely remarking to a neighbour that 'Oor Rab should ha'e had twa wives'.

The affair caused talk in the town, but Burns was unrepentant, celebrating it with a love song, 'The Gowden Locks of Anna':

64

'Yestreen I had a pint o' wine,
A place where body saw na;
Yestreen lay on this breast o' mine
The gowden locks of Anna. . . .'

He was by this time contributing Scottish songs to a collection to be published by George Thomson of Edinburgh. He sent on 'The Gowden Locks of Anna', and when Thomson suggested politely that it might offend public good taste Burns added a defiant last verse:

'The Kirk and State may join an' tell
To do sic things I maunna;
The Kirk and State may gae to h——,
And I'll gae to my Anna.'

Whatever memories and temptations that the Globe stirred, it was to remain his favourite hostelry to the end of his days. It is still in existence, and serving its original purpose. Entry is gained by a narrow lane or close at 56 High Street. The poet's favourite seat is to the right of the fireplace, and his punchbowl and toddy ladle are on display.

Mention has been made of George Thomson and the collection of Scottish songs he was producing in Edinburgh. He had written to Burns asking if he would care to contribute, and the poet had written back enthusiastically. Thomson, a little worried by the poet's fame, wrote back inquiring what fee Burns might expect, only to have his fears allayed by a letter assuring him that 'In the honest enthusiasm with which I embark in your undertaking, to talk of money, wages, fee or hire would be downright prostitution of soul'.

From then till his death Burns poured into Thomson's collection poem after poem without fee. Many of them were inspired by the beautiful countryside surrounding Dumfries, which remained a constant delight to Burns throughout his stay there. Much of the area he knew from his work as an exciseman, which took him past places like Caerlaverock Castle and through the picturesque little ports of the Solway. The rest of it he set out conscientiously to discover—

especially on one memorable trip through the Galloway Highlands with a Dumfries friend, John Syme.

Burns had borrowed a Highland pony for their trip. Their route lay over the wilds of the Galloway Highlands and their first stop was Kenmure Castle, on the banks of the Ken. They were welcomed so heartily by the owners, Mr and Mrs Gordon, that they stayed on for a further two days. In return for the hospitality they had received, Burns wrote an epitaph for Mrs Gordon's lap dog Echo, which had died recently and of which she had been inordinately fond:

'In wood and wild, ye warbling throng,
Your heavy loss deplore;
Now half extinct your powers of song,
Sweet "Echo" is no more. . . .'

Kenmure Castle, now an ivy-clad ruin, can be viewed from the A762 to the south of New Galloway.

From Kenmure Castle Burns and Syme passed through wild and rugged scenery on the moorland road to Gatehouse-on-Fleet. Making it even more wild and rugged was the most spectacular storm either of them had ever seen. Throughout their journey lightning flashed, thunder rolled among the hills, and the rain battered down. Gratefully, they reached Gatehouse, where they put up at the Murray Arms Hotel. One of its proud claims is that Burns wrote 'Scots Wha Hae' there. It is highly probable. Syme records that Burns was lost in thought throughout the thunderstorm, and that he discovered later that the poet had been thinking about Bruce and Bannockburn. Two days later Burns recited the poem to him, and the likeliest place for putting it on paper would have been Gatehouse.

The following morning they travelled to Kirkcudbright, for they had been invited to dine that evening with the Earl of Selkirk in his mansion just outside the town. It was a short, easy journey, but it was given an element of farce by the problem of Burns's new boots. He had bought them specially for the trip, but after their soaking the day before they had dried rock hard and, try as he might, he couldn't get them on his feet. He seems to have been depressed and enraged out of all proportion by the incident, and in the end they rode into Kirkcudbright with Burns's boots slung across Syme's saddle.

They put up at the Selkirk Arms Hotel, where, it is said, Burns wrote the famous Selkirk Grace:

'Some hae meat and canna eat,
And some wad eat that want it:
But we hae meat and we can eat,
Sae let the Lord be thankit.'

Once again this is highly probable, for that evening at the Earl of Selkirk's home at St Mary's Isle, a peninsula running down the east side of Kirkcudbright Bay, Burns was asked to say grace at dinner.

Back in Dumfries Burns had a new—and rather unusual—interest. He had joined the Gentlemen Volunteers. This was the militia, a kind of eighteenth-century Home Guard, pledged to defend the country to the last man should the French ever attempt invasion.

Now that relations with the French had degenerated into open conflict, Burns's early enthusiasm for the revolutionaries had disappeared completely, being replaced by a burning patriotism. He composed a defiant song which exactly caught the mood of the nation, and it was sung everywhere:

'Does haughty Gaul invasion threat?
Then let the louns beware, Sir!
There's WOODEN WALLS upon our seas,
And VOLUNTEERS on shore, Sir:
The *Nith* shall run to *Corsincon*,
And *Criffel* sink in *Solway*
Ere we permit a foreign foe
On British ground to rally!'

The uniform of the Dumfries Volunteers was distinctive and colourful. It is described by a contemporary commentator as consisting of 'white kerseymere breeches and waistcoat; short blue coat, faced with red; and round hat, surmounted by a bearskin, like the helmet of horse-guards'. Burns had himself kitted out by a Dumfries tailor and was inordinately proud of his appearance as he drilled with the other volunteers.

He was not destined, however, to have much use for his colourful new uniform. He was struck down by a severe attack of rheumatic fever and collapsed in the street, lying most of the night until a passer-by, realising he was ill rather than drunk, helped him to his house.

The doctor was called, and Burns was confined to bed indefinitely. It was the end of the Gentlemen Volunteers, of the excise service, of almost every activity. The commanding officer of the Volunteers, himself an amateur rhymer, visited him and tried to rouse him enough to take up poetry-writing again. In a tired verse letter Burns explained the difficulties:

'My honor'd Colonel, deep I feel
Your interest in the Poet's weal:
Ah! now sma' heart hae I to speel
The steep Parnassus
Surrounded thus by bolus pill
And potion glasses.'

Only once was his muse to flare up again. His wife, Jean, was again pregnant, and to help with the nursing of Burns the sister of an excise colleague, Jessie Lewars, was called in. She was an attractive young woman, and that heart, which the poet himself had once described as 'tinder', caught fire for the last time. He called for pen and paper and wrote for her one of his tenderest love songs:

'Oh, wert thou in the cauld blast,
On yonder lea, on yonder lea,
My plaidie to the angry airt,
I'd shelter thee, I'd shelter thee;
Or did Misfortune's bitter storms
Around thee blaw, around thee blaw,
Thy bield should be my bosom,
To share it a', to share it a'.'

Later Mendelssohn set the words to music.

68

Burns eventually left his sick bed, but he was far from recovered. After a slight improvement his condition deteriorated rapidly, and eventually, in desperation, his doctor recommended sea-bathing. He suggested a little resort on the Solway Firth called Brow Well, because, as well as affording sea-bathing, it also possessed a spring which was thought to have medicinal properties.

If we leave Dumfries by the road which today passes the Crichton Royal Institution, we can follow Burns on his last despairing journey in search of health. The road passes through the picture postcard resort of Glencaple, then sweeps on past the ruins of Caerlaverock Castle. Beyond Bankend and just before the village of Ruthwell the hamlet of Brow Well is reached—a couple of houses by the roadside. By the roadside, too, is the famous mineral spring, now only a trickle of dark brown water, but with a tablet bearing the inscription: 'The Brow Well visited by the poet Burns, July 1796.'

Just beside the well is a gate which leads down to the shore. Modern medical opinion believes that Burns's heart had been badly affected by rheumatic fever, and that sea-bathing was tantamount to suicide, but here, each day for two weeks, the poet obediently paddled out till the water was lapping round his armpits, then struggled back to lie panting and near collapse on the pebbly beach.

As he lay there he had other things to worry him besides his health. One of his last letters was written to George Thomson, the publisher to whom he had contributed so many songs without any thought of payment. It doesn't make comfortable reading:

'After all my boasted independence, curst necessity compels me to implore you for five pounds. A cruel haberdasher, to whom I owe an account, taking it into his head that I am dying, has commenced a process and will infallibly put me into jail. Do, for God's sake, send me that sum, and that by return of post. Forgive me this earnestness; but the horrors of a jail have made me half-distracted.'

The account was for the militia uniform of which he had been so touchingly proud in his days with the Dumfries Volunteers. To soften the demand he enclosed with his letter the manuscript of 'Fairest Maid on Devon Bank', which dated back to his love affair with Peggy Chalmers at Harvieston. He also promised, once he had recovered, to send Thomson a parcel of the finest lyrics that he, Thomson, would ever see.

At the same time he sent off a similar letter to his cousin, James Burnes of Montrose, whom he had met in happier circumstances. The letter ends with the following words:

'O, James! did you know the pride of my heart, you would feel doubly for me! Alas! I am not used to beg! O, do not disappoint me! Save me from the horrors of a jail!'

In a letter to his friend Cunningham he gives an insight into the cause of all his financial troubles, the fact that during his long illness he had been unable to undertake his excise duties. The letter ends with the plea:

'I beg of you to use your utmost interest, and that of all your friends, to move our Commissioners of Excise to grant me my full salary. If they do not grant it . . . if I die not of disease, I must perish with hunger.'

The Excise, be it said to their shame, refused the request.

By now it had become clear that as a cure the visit to Brow Well had been in vain. At the end of two weeks he was so ill that he could not mount a horse, and had to be carried back to Dumfries in a cart. Visitors to his house today will notice immediately that it is built halfway up a slight brae, and on that July day in 1796 passers-by were horrified to see that Burns had to go on all fours to negotiate it. When he entered the house worse was to follow. Jean, her pregnancy run almost full course, had already been put to bed. In desperation Burns wrote off to his father-in-law, begging him to send Mrs Armour to Dumfries. He then went to his bed in the other room.

In the next three days a stream of visitors called, but Burns was beyond receiving them. He rallied once. Opening his eyes to find some of his friends from the Gentlemen Volunteers looking down at him anxiously, he grinned and remarked wrily: "Dinna let the awkward squad fire over me!"

They were his last recorded words. He died on the 21st July 1796, at the age of thirty-seven.

Dumfries, which had provided so little financial help during his ten months' illness, spared no expense with his funeral. Still jutting out into the centre of High Street, and slowing the twentieth-century traffic, is the historic Mid-Steeple. It was there his body was taken for the official lying-in-state on the day before the funeral. It was from here too that the impressive cortège set out. The body was borne by the Gentlemen Volunteers, who provided the guard of honour. All the leading dignitaries of the town and county followed in procession, and the streets were lined by detachments of the Angus Fencibles and the Cinque Ports Cavalry.

The route took them past Burns's house, and at almost the moment they were passing Jean gave birth to a son. A little later the long procession reached its destination, St Michael's Church, where Burns had worshipped and where his pew is now carefully marked by a plaque. As the burial took place, and as the military salute rang out in 'three ragged and straggling volleys', many must have remembered the poet's last words.

A little diligent searching will take the visitor to the original grave, provided, like the modest original tombstone, by the family. The poet was not, however, to be allowed to remain there very long. His fame convinced the nation that something a little more imposing was called for in St Michael's Churchyard, and in 1815 his body was removed to a specially constructed marble mausoleum depicting the Muse casting her mantle over him as he worked in the fields with his plough.

There was to be yet one more disturbance of the grave

71

before he was finally allowed to rest in peace. In 1834 his widow Jean died, and when the grave was opened in preparation for her funeral, scientists dug up Burns's skull and took plaster casts of it to see whether the science of phrenology could provide from the measurements of his skull any reason for his genius. Visitors interested in such gruesome details will find a plaster cast of the skull on display in the museum at the rear of the cottage at Alloway.

Since his death Burns has been generously treated by Scotland. No poet has been more honoured by any nation. Every year on the anniversary of his birth Burns Suppers are held at which thousands of his countrymen solemnly drink toasts to his immortal memory.

For the poet, unfortunately, it came a little late, and reading that last distracted correspondence from Brow Well, you find it difficult, despite all the present-day adulation, not to echo Burns's own bitter lines written about the neglect of another poet:

'My curse upon your whunstane hearts,
Ye Enbrugh gentry!
The tythe o' what ye waste at cartes
Wad stow'd his pantry!'

A Burns Chronology

1759 Robert Burns born in Alloway on 25th January.

1766 Family moves to the farm of Mount Oliphant.

1773 Composes first poem, 'Handsome Nell'.

1775 Sent to Kirkoswald to learn mensuration, surveying, etc.

1777 Family moves to the farm of Lochlea, near Tarbolton.

1780 Starts, in conjunction with some friends, the Bachelors' Club in Tarbolton.

1781 Sent to Irvine to learn flax-dressing.

1784 Death of his father. Family moves to farm of Mossgiel, near Mauchline.

1786 Burns's form of marriage to Jean Armour repudiated by her father.
Betrothal to 'Highland' Mary Campbell, with whom he intends to emigrate.
Death of Mary Campbell.
Publication of first edition (Kilmarnock Edition) of his works.
Burns goes to Edinburgh.

1787 Publication of Edinburgh edition of his works.
Border tour with Robert Ainslie.
First Highland tour.
Second Highland tour.
Third Highland tour (Peggy Chalmers tour).
Meets Clarinda (Mrs Agnes Maclehose).

1788   Returns to Mauchline.
        Marries Jean Armour.
        Takes farm of Ellisland, near Dumfries.

1789   Burns appointed to Excise.

1790   Writes *Tam O' Shanter*.

1791   Gives up Ellisland and moves to Dumfries.

1794   Moves from the Bank Vennel, Dumfries, to Mill Brae
        (now Burns Street).
        Makes tour of Galloway Highlands with Syme of
        Ryedale.

1796   Struck down with rheumatic fever.
        To Brow Bell in vain attempt to regain health.
        Burns dies in Dumfries on 21st July.

Reading List

Bawdy Burns, Cyril Pearl (London, 1958).

The Burns Encyclopedia, Maurice Lindsay, 2nd revised edition (London, 1970).

Discovering the Burns Country, Andrew Fergus (Great Britain, 1976).

The Letters of Robert Burns, Edited by J. DeLancey Ferguson, 2 vols (Oxford, 1931).

The Life of Robert Burns, Catherine Carswell (London, 1931).

The Life of Robert Burns, F. B. Snyder (New York, 1932).

The Merry Muses and Other Burnsian Frolics (London, 1966).

Poetical Works of Robert Burns, Edited by William Wallace (London and Edinburgh).

Portrait of the Burns Country, Hugh Douglas, 3rd edition (London, 1975).

Pride and Passion: Robert Burns, 1759-1796, J. DeLancey Ferguson (New York, 1939).

Robert Burns, Hans Hecht (translated by Jane Lymburn), 2nd revised edition (London, 1950).

Robert Burns and His World, David Daiches (London, 1971).